List for contents of TRE/

About the Book

Dedication

About the Author

About the book

TREASURED is an insightful collection of poems, and is the sequel to Touching Things In Time. The incredibly poignant tale of my survival. May you be moved.

I chose the title " TREASURED", as I feel it is deeply rooted in the uniqueness of everything that life offers.

The tree image on the front cover was constructed out of a variety of recycled materials. The back cover blends digital art and fabric. The overall image symbolises a butterfly's lifecycle in the hope of a new beginning

Waste not, want not. Is a core philosophy in my art making process . I am a firm believer that even scraps may create an effective impact.

It is my hope that all my readers will find pearls within these pages that resonate with them,.to incorporate into their daily lives.

"Books are pockets lined with wisdom."

Dedication

Treasured is dedicated to my late and loyal mobility dog Cassie, who sadly passed away in 2020. I am truly blessed to have had her by my side for 12 years. During which time she constantly acted as an extra set of arms and legs for me. My sincere thanks to Mobility Assistance Dogs for enabling me to have " unleashed life", an unforgettably life changing journey

My heartfelt thanks to all my family and friends for their support in making my experience the success that it was.

I wrote an acrostic poem "Cassie",as my personal tribute for the many years of service she gave me after her passing.

Her spirit still continues to leave its mark imprinted on my life .

Touching Things in Time

Treasured memories

Observe finer details with insight

Uplifting

Chance to exercise creative expression

Harmony between words and images

Increase in knowledge, expands my life's appetite

Nourishing to mental state

Genuine though short

Together with words we become one, reader and writer

Happenings throughout

Intelligence shared

Not long, still deep

Generally based on my life story

Sentimental

Innovative

New perspective illustrated

Topics real, sometimes brutal

Instrumental in altering my life for the better

Momentous in expressing significant life events

Evolutionary in dealing with life adversity

Book

Touching things in time

Words that rhyme

Grow and show my life

Through poems

Idea

Palette shapes wide smile with envelope in pattern shade ,
deliberate sprawl all over in order to bleed carnage,

Depicts various paths undertaken, destined for killer victory

Decisive plan to immerse itself in emerald sea green eye of
rebirth is the mane focal point

Time stretches where it shell reach home to wise depths of
intuition

Theatrical nature centred around exuberant warmth on the
conscience of a lion's heart.

Novel

Finger through the pages, like walk

through the forest

Absorbing the unique wisdom each

environment has to offer

Great blessings and insights

Novel idea

Pack

Hunter taken down for blood and bone

Eyes bright illuminate night

Green go start fight

Blanket encompasses organ preservation

In golden attire

Pause meticulous to mark plan

Mental might fierce enough To alliterate victim

Lion

Roar

Stamp

Enveloped in protection of self and other

Built on knowledge and lessons learnt

To top it off and seal the deal

Serenity

A web of success

Created by waves and seas

Bringing peace to both mind and heart

Persona like a lion

GROWL

Gentle from the inside out

Ready always

Optimistic

Willingness to protest, without doubt

Love is ubiquitous

Heaven

From a dark place as black as an unkempt grave,

Tied to the ground

Concrete in completion

Stars in the night sky, flicker electricity on

Chills to the core, dead

Of no particular definition

Photographic memories produced, hoped for in next life,

Snowflake

Sky's ice falling

Concrete in holding its own

Unique shape

Stamps its mark on earth like a footprint

Cassie.

Compassionately contented soul with an

unwavering willingness to assist, always

ready to do her best

amazing creature with an admirable

attitude and personality

strong spirit combining a soft nature both

inside and out

still with and protecting me from the shelf

intimate-times shared and memories

made during working and retired life

enduring loyalty as well as love from

and for everyone who was blessed to know

her

Message

I write this letter to you to help you gain a fresh perspective about what happened to Cassie through the knowledge that she is now with the stars at night and clouds in the day. I now have a clear vision of opinion. This makes it possible for me to be at peace, and not cry rivers or tears. Through the art of acceptance I realise even though these days she has left her shell to live in paradise. Her spirit remains strong in heart and mind. Thanks so much Luke for the time we shared such deep bravery. This taught us both a moment lesson about how precious life can be in its fragility.

Love Onie X

Grave

Today again I stare into the lonely abyss of grief.

Again I source healing by connecting to the divine

power of spirituality.

Physically I wait for the right time to meet again,

when I too will reach the highest realm of tranquility

in heaven.

Vanished

Gone from sight, with all my might

Life rebuilt

A new

Reveal

New beginnings

Come from endings

The surprise of either

Is layered underneath

Waiting to be opened

Intricate

Various shades of coloured texture

Constructed in the metallic fashion as a tree

Quotation forms canopy to nourish flow, leaves

nothing unsaid and done

Central to invested memories

Draped in a sea of wisdom

So I take a look at mine

Read the fine print "a wise mind is the root to

a lion's heart ".

Dainty doll

Tree

From the heavens

Down to earth

Energy flows from me to you

and you to me

As an overall source of connection grows,like an umbilical cord

Strong

Born

Dive into life

Even when in strife

You might surprise yourself

With your ability to rise

Up, up, up

Grow

Black, red, white

With all might

Glow with the flow

Shine bright at night

Mark Maori sovereignty

Identity

An eighth Samoan,happens to be part of my heritage

The Pacific portion, passed down from generation to

generation

A small, yet significant piece of my identity

Land,sea and ancestry. a big part of community

Being a part of them, and them part of me,

Is what is important to me

Makes me proud to belong

to a Pacific community

Embracing this identity

gifts me a sense of cultural security

Whether

The dawn breaks

Grounded in a sacred desire

The inner and outer worlds

Rinsed clean with a common

Sense of familiarity

Waiting for the next rotation

Cycle is complete

Bottomless

War is the home of death

depicting negative uncertainty

its core purpose

blues creating waves which makes me think of walking

away,

I watch the tv with

scrutiny hoping for

inspiration,

to prevail

to no avail

Doodling

Images emerge from an imagination

running rampant

Like a volcano erupting with decoration,

rather than debris

Creativity

Art is the happy part

Of the heart

So go with the flow

Let your grow

Shine bright

And you'll be right

Start

Make art

From the heart

Let go

Flow

Where it goes you will know

Matariki

Marvel as colours fill the sky, like a warm winter blanket

Alternate between clouds, sun, moon and stars

Togetherness emphasised

Auric field energy randomly constant

Radiant light, ever so bright

Intricate details traced with imagination

Kindred spirits permanently bonded through time and space

Instrumental in creation of entire constellation

Star World

Various mediums combine

Inner and outer world

through creativity

What a star

System

Sun, moon and stars all combine

Solar power across the sky

Each with its own individual function Illuminate

the heavens like electricity provides light to our home,

Here on earth

Whole

Art is a wheel

Colour at its core

Swirling effects build the possibility for opportunity

forging an ever changing society, allowing for long

lasting impact

Despite wheels being central to my physicality.

I still exercise my senses through a photographic

memory

Being different continuously spins my life's wheel.

Expanding my mind into free and open oceans of

expression, resolving and dissolving societal limitations

Rainbow

Curves decorate the sky

Prisms of heavenly light

Shine bright

We bow our head in grace, giving thanks to the divine

Gratitude saturates our heart with loving rain

We bow in prayer

Amen

Deposit

To give what I can

When I can

In whatever ways I can

I am grateful

The rewards plentiful in resources

Rather than money

I can be the change I wish to transfer into this world

Offerings always accepted with thanks

Celebrate

Presents as gifts, or presence of people

Each holds its own weight in bring uniquely.precious

Generations gathered

A treasured memory

Worthy of time taken to celebrate

Holiday

Break in routine usual

No schedule needed

Entertainment required

Education relaxed

Vacation places different

Higher volumes of people and traffic

Chaos still very much alive

Have a blast while it lasts

Return

Back to belonging

Complete again

Health renewed

Gorgeous Day

A beautiful day

Keeps the doctor away

By keeping bugs at bay

Be sure to absorb a ray of sunshine

Have a great day

Unreal

Fantasy land

On a grand scale

Makes my life not bland

Room to bloom with mixture of sights and sounds

Credit given to Walt Disney

Fish

Eyes like googles

Reflects wave of self image

Mirrors quality of tranquility from land and sea

Kingyo chochin

With deep gratitude

We celebrate the tenderness of your light

Sense of community

Echoes through the streets

As the intricate details

Of such a precious icon

Is always seen to be spinning

In reflection

Of its own, unique solitude

Central to the value

Of the city

Yanai

Cloud

A thought bubble

Rising from my imagination

Like ashes from an extinguished fire

Still warms my heart with the Earth's embrace

Drying up all storms of tension

United as one

Surface

Colour of climate

Bold with variation

Mixed together in blends of protection

Shading us from scarcity

Under the umbrella of unity

Linking us together as one

Propelling us forward in a circular motion

Driven into whichever world we belong

Benefitting from the wheel of continuous prosperity

Well

Fear, anger, hatred and suffering

all dissolved into calmness

like a cloud having its moisture extracted

leaving a blanketed layer of peace behind

waking up to a brighter day

when we will rise again

oh the relief

Amen

Waterfall

Leaving home fills my heart with sacred brokenness

My consciousness gingerly floats away

Leaving all my thoughts and feelings to scatter at random

As I ponder where to next

Then in the distant darkness of my dream

I subtly travel in the safe direction of downstream

Gently awakened by the light

Leaving me in awe

As my. sense of wonder is rightfully illuminated

Like a mirror reflecting a tranquil waterfall

Overflowing with the seasoned. current of everlasting change

Piece

Woven into mix

A finishing touch rustles

Naturally blends

Reminder

Remembering to play after life's storms

Keeps the doctor away

Develops the immunity

Of a soldier

Determined by a peace

Of

Happiness

Picture

Drawn from experience

Objective and subjective

Full of colour, textured with pattern

Creates a peaceful environment for a brighter day

Energised motion

Loneliness is the weakness of being alone in contrast solitude is the strength

Grounded in Beauty

Colours meshed together

While leaves sway like a pendulum,

and resonate with the unwrapping of

crepe paper on Christmas Day

Chrysalis

Cross cultural elements

Bring forth a star

Love and rejuvenating emerges

From those near and far

Butterfly

Fly high towards the sky

Propelled forward by wings, flight light

May we meet again when this journey

Called little comes to an end

When all our problems will mend

Blessings until then

Being

Butterfly, a transformative symbol

From the insect world,like buddha

from the spiritual world

Everlasting life

Grief

Lost in the depths of a dark city my thoughts are

clouds of confusion

While I stare out the window and watch the lush

hills over a bright sunshine

A combination of confusion and uncertainty helps

me to rebuild the foundation of my house when I return

Empty

Even though my heart is sad

I feel glad to share every little piece of it with others

Surrounding them with rays of sunshine

Emits a protective light when facing what feels like

an uncertain dark night.

Thanks for the might

Roar

Opening

Flowers fresh or fake

It is unknown

Arranged here and there

With an ikebana flare

Candle flame burns a new life

Live courageously

Keep memories combined in mind and heart, alive

Like a lotus already seen from where we have been, still forever

Emerging with possibilities

About the Author

I am an artist who enjoys the freedom and flow associated with painting. This is especially important to me, not only as a person, but also to my creative process because it breaks down the barriers connected to living with Cerebral Palsy.(CP). I use an electric wheelchair to assist with my mobility.

In recent years I have had hours of fun exploring the digital art scene. This has greatly improved my autonomy with art making. I have even been able to turn my digital drawings from an image into merchandise. My products are available to view and purchase on my website. (http://www.leonie86.digitees.co.nz)

I have also expanded my craft with writing through my blog Growl, which focuses on poetry.(www.frizzydome.wordpress.com)

I wish to extend my deepest gratitude to Mapura Studios for all their support in "making my creativity become reality."

It is a wheel blessing to have the support of all my readers.

" May your thoughts and feelings fly high into the sky like a butterfly. Giving you a seamless life line."

Milton Keynes UK
Ingram Content Group UK Ltd.
UKHW021540120924
448244UK00011B/332

9 798331 059415